"Christian Counseling

Teaching Tools"

DIVINE
DIALOGUE
PART 4

Discipling
DYNAMICS

"I WILL INSTRUCT THEE AND TEACH THEE IN THE WAY WHICH THOU SHALT GO; I WILL GUIDE THEE WITH MINE EYE."

PSALM 32:8

JOHN F. GILLETTE
Author of Pastoral Health Care Series

Chapbook Press

Schuler Books
2660 28th Street SE
Grand Rapids MI 49512

www.schulerbooks.com/chapbook-press

Discipling Dynamics

Copyright ©2021 — Dr. John F. Gillette, Ph.D., D. Min.

All rights reserved. Published 2021.

Printed at Schuler Books, Chapbook Press, Grand Rapids, Michigan, in the United States of America.

Distribution contact:at jjgillette@comcast.net.

ISBN 13: 9781948237802

Library of Congress Control Number: 2021908042

Cover photo: Pexels.com

Printed in the United States of America

John Gillette's writings flow from a lifetime of experience. It is one thing to write out of a knowledge based on research. It is an entirely different thing to write out of a depth of life experience. John has both. As a pastor who has cared for the needs of a congregation, as a husband who has experienced the tragic loss of a wife, and as a child of God who has walked through the joys and pain of following the Lord, John has so much to offer in this series. From the opening pages, through to the very end, you will be blessed by the insights, loving tone and encouragement you receive from this series. God has used John greatly in ministry and will continue to use him through this life-giving series.

—Josh Mateer, D. Min.

True, illustrative, practical stories are like windows that unlock Bible truths and promises. Along with a masterfully orchestrated short stories should come the truth that God's Word and love has been experienced by His servants as they partner with Him in the work of rebuilding the Kingdom. A gifted teacher, Dr. Gillette lives an ordinary life abiding in Christ and being an obedient servant of the Lord. As he sees God working in his life, and in the lives of those to whom he ministers, his faith is refreshed and he is encouraged to press on through life's uncertainties.

Only a lifetime dedicated to nurturing, ministering, teaching, and keen insight through the power of the Holy Spirit, can produce such poignant stories that teach and challenge.

—Mulonge M. Kalumbula, Ph.D.

John's books give us hope and light. He reminds us that through Jesus we are never alone. I have certainly needed that reminder in my life and in my practice. In holding a patient's hand, and helping them through a condition or disease, reminding them that they are never alone has become the greatest gift of health care.

—Linda M. Kunce, D.C.

The series reminds me that Jesus knows what it's like to live in a human body. I have received Jesus and His forgiveness, but as the book suggests, I also have the power from the Holy Spirit. His books have encouraged me to gain courage through prayer and confidence in Jesus to meet my needs. John's honesty is very special to read as he reflects on his own life and struggles. I like his explanation that "the soul is where the emotions are and the mind is where the thinking takes place". It's been good for me to read that God works through weakness, and learn that John found God with him in the middle of the struggles.

—*Arvid W. Vandyke, Ed.D.*

Discovering God's Counsel is a book full of great spiritual truths from someone who has developed a very close and deep relationship with Jesus through his life. John provides a meaningful and inspirational testimony, with examples from his own experiences, of how relying on God's Word and promises can give you the power, hope, and peace you need to overcome life's struggles and challenges. The Scriptures he chose in his book were on point and helpful. It was an enjoyable and wonderful read.

—*Thoa Reyna, J.D.*

John has written a user-friendly and practical series for anyone desiring to live beyond the superficial and venture into the supernatural. The world needs this *Pastoral Health Care Series*. Pastors and followers of Jesus need the insights from John's lifetime experience of walking with God and caring for His people through the power of the Holy Spirit. John has brilliantly show that God is enough, God's love is real, God's counsel is enduring, and God reigns supremely. This important series will serve both the church and the world for many years to come.

—*Kizombo Kalumbula, Jr., Ph.D.*

John Gillette's inspirational book *Glorify God* is a fantastic reminder of how I should approach each day and how blessed I am. It is so easy to get caught up in the hustle and bustle of today's lifestyle and forget what is really important. John's encouraging words are a great reminder of how we all should live each day. I have a great foundation of faith nut John's book helps me to remember what is important and allows me to reflect on the wonderful things I have and to be gracious to God for those blessings.

— *Tammy Thelen, Au.D., CCC-A*

Note from the Author

I believe in God's sovereignty and compassion. I am learning to let go of self and to hold onto someone that can do whatever he pleases. Sometimes life is cruel, sometimes it is full of suffering, physically and psychologically. A spiritual solution to meet difficult trials has become my goal. God's Word carries with it no uncertainties. I want it to saturate my mind and heart..

The *Pastoral Health Care Series* and *Divine Dialogue Series* was created through unexpected heart disease (open heart surgery), cancer (medication and surgery), a stroke and major head injury after a car accident that also resulted in the death of my wife.

It is helping me to develop and adequate level to supernatural, psychological and physical adjustments. It may help you as well. It has brought me security.

—*John F. Gillette, D.S.M., D.Min*

Discipling
DYNAMICS

Other Books by John Gillette:

Discovering God's Sufficiency
Going Beyond Ourselves and Experiencing the Supernatural
Pastoral Health Care —Part One

Discovering God's Love
Confirming God's Love through the evidence of historical facts
Pastoral Health Care — Part Two

Discovering God's Counsel
Applying his spiritual solution to meet difficult trials
Pastoral Health care — Part Three

Discovering God's Kingdom
Finding a way to understand ourselves in a complex world
Pastoral Health Care — Part Four

Discovering God's Heart
Finding God's heart pulse is our daily challenge
Pastoral Health Care — Part Five

Glorify God
Christianity is a divine vitality
Divine Dialogue — Part One

Dynamic Doer
Biblical Christianity is Jesus Christ
Divine Dialogue — Part Two

Satisfying Strength
Biblical meditation works. Allow Psalms to sweep you into all directions.
Divine Dialogue — Part Three

Discipling Dynamics
Christian counseling teaching tool
Divine Dialogue — Part Four

Triplets' Trilogy
A spiritual autobiography of praise, promise and prayer.
Divine Dialogue — Part Five

This book is dedicated to Senior Leadership, Board of Directors, and staff of the Kalamazoo Gospel Ministries that live beyond the superficial and venture into the supernatural. God is enough, God's love is real, God's counsel is enduring and God reigns supremely.

Index

Anger
Appropriation
Authority
Our Choice
Our Contentment
Our Counseling
Our Decisions
Depression
Our Description
Our Enablement
The Enemy
Our Faith
Fear
Feeling Inferior
Our Feelings
Our Gifts
Our God
The Gospel
Our Guide
Our Impossibilities

Our Mind
Our Personal Development
Our Christian Philosophy
Our Praise
Our Promises
Our Power
Our Responsibility
Our Reward
Satan
Our Sin
Our Spiritual Battles
Our Spiritual Warfare
Our Suffering
Our Sufficiency
Overcoming Addictions
The Sure Cure
Our Testimony
Our Trials
Warfare
Our Worship

I would like to ACKNOWLEDGE the need to write these brochures for my own spiritual development. They have become a priority in my daily journey.

I APPRECIATE all the people that God has used to influence me. Many of these thoughts that have come to my mind over the past sixty years are through sermons, lectures, communications, meditations and readings. Everyone I have come in contact with should be given credit.

I hope the brochures can be used to assist in our caring for the people.

I give ADORATION to our Lord Jesus Christ through what I have learned and will continue to learn through these homework assignments.

ANGER

A quick-tempered man displays folly.

Proverbs 14:29

christian counseling teaching tools

What is anger?

Anger is our response to hurt or fear.

Anger is not always negative. It can be justified in some situations. Anger becomes a problem when it controls one's actions and thoughts.

Anger can be a defense. Sometimes it is the only way a person knows how to deal with an uncomfortable or painful situation. If this is the case in your life, resolve to take Jesus as your Lord. Although your anger may seem overwhelming, it can be managed by developing a self-controlled lifestyle.

Developing Self-Control

1. Choose to put on the new self (Ephesians 4:22–24). How can you accomplish this in your life?

2. Take conscious control of your thought life.

    Refuse to let your thoughts go down the usual path (Proverbs 14:29).

    Try to see how God is seeking to use the situation to help you grow (Romans 12:20–21).

    Let self-control become instructive (Ephesians 4:29–32).

3. Develop a new perspective: love the unlovely.

    Develop a sense of dignity: cultivate your significance.

    Develop a sense of humor: practice joy daily.

When you are faced with a potentially explosive situation, practice the following steps:

- Analyze the situation: Take honest responsibility for yourself.
- Deliberately reject thoughts of retaliating: Don't repay anyone for evil.
- Plan a constructive confrontation: Heal the problem.
- Disarm anger with forgiveness: Practice the fruits of the Spirit.

Think of a time of a recent outburst of your anger. Write an evaluation of the situation using the steps above.

1. What happened? Who did what and who said what?

2. How did you respond?

3. How could you have healed the situation—either during the confrontation or right after?

4. What fruit of the Spirit applies to this situation? (See Galatians 5:22–23).

Now that you have worked through this assignment, what do you want to see as the next step?

Notes adapted from Peter Wilkes, Overcoming Anger. Intervarsity Press: 1987.

John F. Gillette, Ph.D.

APPROPRIATION

Grace to help us in our time of need.

Hebrews 4:16

christian counseling teaching tools

WHAT DOES *APPROPRIATE* MEAN?

The basic meaning of the word *appropriate* is to "take possession." We take possession of the divine strength God has made available to us in Christ.

Follow these steps when you read the next Scripture passage.

1. Interpret the text. Ask questions about each part of the verse.

2. Ask yourself what principles from the text you can apply to your life.

3. Memorize a verse and recite it each day.

4. Respond to what you have read by writing a note of thanks to God, journaling your thoughts, or recording your questions.

READ HEBREWS 4:15–16

1. Interpret the text by meditating on these questions:

Who is our high priest?

How does he sympathize with weakness?

How was he tempted in every way?

How can we approach the throne of grace with confidence?

How can we receive mercy/find grace?

What is your greatest need right now?

2. What are some principles from this passage that you can apply to your life?

3. Choose a verse from the passage to memorize this week.

4. Respond to your study by writing down your thoughts and questions.

God has given us his strength. Read the following Scriptures, one for each day for the rest of this week.
Work through each passage using the four-step plan shown on the previous pages.

Psalm 79:8–13

Philippians 4:11–19

Matthew 6:5–15

1 Peter 4:7–19

Romans 8:1–17

John 15:1–17

Now that you have worked through this assignment, what do you want to see as the next step?

Notes taken from Jerry Bridges, Transforming Grace. NavPress: 1990, p. 171.

John F. Gillette, Ph.D.

OUR AUTHORITY

Every Sabbath he reasoned in the synagogue, trying to persuade Jews and Greeks. So Paul stayed for a year and half, teaching them the word of God.

Acts 18:4,11

christian counseling teaching tools

The authority of the Scriptures continues through the teaching of the Word. You can reason and persuade people, but Scripture is a living, vital agency with supernatural power in itself. The Bible says,

> As the rain and the snow
>   come down from heaven,
> and do not return to it
>   without watering the earth
> and making it bud and flourish,
>   so that it yields seed for the sower and bread for the eater,
>
> so is my word that goes out from my mouth:
>   It will not return to me empty,
> but will accomplish what I desire
>   and achieve the purpose for which I sent it.
> (Isaiah 55:10–11)

And in the book of Jeremiah, God says, " 'Is not my word like fire,' declares the LORD, 'and like a hammer that breaks a rock in pieces?' " (23:29).

God has given his Word so that believers may grow (see 1 Peter 2:2).

We haven't fulfilled our obligations to the Word until application has taken place. The Bible is not only the source book for information, but it has life-changing power for what we face every day.

Read James 1:25 and John 12:17. What is to be our response to the Word?

Read Hebrews 4:12. How does the Word affect our lives?

Read 2 Timothy 3:16–17. What does the Word do for us?

Read Psalm 119:1. What results from our reading the Word?

The Bible realistically and sufficiently meets our deepest problems, longings, needs, and inadequacies. It provides answers for our need for deliverance from the penalty of sin. It guides us in spiritual progress, helps us in daily victory, and leads our personal relationships and conduct. As we learn more about the Bible, it can help us in all our daily activities.

Consider memorizing a verse every day this year. At the end of the year, you'll have 365 verses in your heart and mind. If that seems too much at first, try memorizing a verse every week. The Word of God will bring about happiness, direction, peace, and contentment. Pray about every verse you memorize.

As you memorize a verse, pray about it. Let the verse become a part of your being and life. When you see the promises of God fulfilled in your life, record those times of God's work.

And also, pass it on! Talk about what you are memorizing. Tell others of the peace you have found. Tell them of the promises you see fulfilled in your life.

When you walk in the law of the Lord, you will find purpose and peace.

John F. Gillette, Ph.D.

OUR CHOICE

I want to remind you of the gospel I preached to you . . .
that Christ died for our sins according to the Scriptures,
that he was buried, that he was raised on the third day
according to the Scriptures.

1 Corinthians 15:1, 3–4

christian counseling teaching tools

What is the Gospel?

The gospel is the "Good News," the news that Christ died for us and rose again for our sins. Why is the news so good? Well, the Good News makes a new person out of you. You cannot change on your own. You cannot enter heaven on your own. You cannot live a full and complete life on your own.

If you respond with your mind and heart to the gospel, you will see a change in your life.

I have studied different religions, human nature, and my own behavior, and I have realized that the gospel is the only answer to the challenges of human existence. Jesus Christ is the only way.

What does the Bible say about the Good News?

"According to the Scriptures"
With careful study of the evidence, we can have confidence that the Bible is God's Word. There is no doubt in my mind that it is. Let it speak to for itself. Get rid of any doubts and destructive thoughts, find a quiet place, and begin to read. You will be surprised how the words will apply to your life.

"Christ died for our sins"
God, the supernatural being, created the heavens and earth. He created humans and loved us so much that he gave his Son to die for us. Jesus Christ, the Son of God, became our substitute for the penalty of sins. Sin is rebellion against God. It doesn't matter if you are wicked person or a good, hard-working citizen, you have inherited a sinful nature because of the disobedience of the first humans, Adam and Eve. It may not seem fair, but we do not measure up to God's standards of holiness and perfection. The only way to be accepted by God is to believe that Christ carried our sins to the grave and experienced the punishment that we deserved when he died. He took upon himself the judgement meant for humans. We have been forgiven and set free by God when we believe the gospel news.

"He was raised on the third day"
In Christ's resurrection, the believer has power to do what God wants. In believing, you have been given a new nature (1 Corinthians 6:11). But you have to choose to believe. It must be deliberate choice.

Meditate on these words from the Bible this week. What choice will you make?

Faith is a decision to entrust ourselves to something or someone. Do you have faith in a chair when you sit on it? Do you have faith in an amusement park ride when you board it? Biblical faith operates in much the same way. We have to put our faith in God into action and believe.

We have learned the facts concerning our sin, and it demands a personal response. I had to make a decision to believe what God had to say and to trust Jesus Christ as my only hope for forgiveness and eternal life (John 10:9; Acts 20:21). It has been the most important decision of my life. Have you made that choice? If not, just pray:

Dear God,
I know that I am a sinner. I believe that you sent your Son to die on the cross to pay the penalty for my sin. I put my faith in you and trust you completely. Come into my heart and control my life.
Thank you, Lord.

If you prayed that prayer, you can be assured that you are now a Christian. Contact me, and I will help you grow in your new life!

John F. Gillette, Ph.D.

OUR CONTENTMENT

> I have learned to be content whatever the circumstances. I know what it is to be in need, and I know what it is to have plenty. I have learned the secret of being content in any and every situation, whether well fed or hungry, whether living in plenty or in want.
>
> *Philippians 4:11–12*

christian counseling teaching tools

What does it mean to be content in all circumstances? What could Paul be talking about?

Paul had been through many trials. He had been stoned, shipwrecked, beaten, rejected by his enemies and hurt by his friends. Yet Paul found peace through it all. What does *content* mean? First, it does not mean relying on ourselves. It doesn't mean finding "inner strength." Paul relied on the strength of Christ, and that is what we need to do.

Contentment is not based on possessions or position. Contentment lies in a relationship with Jesus Christ. Through that relationship and understanding of God's purpose for our lives, we can face any circumstance successfully.

What circumstances are you facing where you need contentment?

Read Romans 8:28. What does this verse tell you about God and his plans for you?

Read Philippians 4:13. How can you face your difficult circumstances?

Read 1 Timothy 1:12. How do you feel the strength of God in your life?

Now consider your situation thoughtfully. How can you face your circumstances with knowledge about contentment?

Think of one difficult circumstance in your life right now. Write it below.

How can you have peace in this circumstance?

Where will you get your power?

What does that power do for you to change your approach to the circumstance?

Spend some time thanking God for his power and peace.

Now that you have worked through this assignment, what do you want to see as the next step?

John F. Gillette, Ph.D.

Our Counseling

> And in the church God has appointed first of all apostles, second prophets, third teachers, then workers of miracles, also those having gifts of healing, those able to help others.
>
> *1 Corinthians 12:28*

christian counseling teaching tools

Biblical (nouthetic) counseling works by means of the Holy Spirit to bring about change in the personality and behavior of the counselee. It works for both immediate and long-term problems. It consists of teaching, discussion, and change through practicing the principles of Scriptures. It involves confession, repentance, and the development of the new biblical patterns. It includes love from a pure heart and a good conscience, and a sincere faith. Read through the following guidelines for those wishing to help others.

Be Biblical

Acts 20:31	Warn others
2 Corinthians 11:29	Help those who are weak
Ephesians 4:15,29	Speak truth
Colossians 3:16–17	Admonish others
1 Thessalonians 2:7–9	Be gentle
3 John 1:4	Walk in the truth

Be Available
Become involved
Become sensitive to the needs of others
Display your value-system
Take people seriously
Confront the problem
Be alert regarding manipulation
Model behavior
Don't ramble
Be solution-oriented

Be Specific
Include a complete personal data inventory
Let questions grow out of the facts received
Listen carefully
Withhold judgement
Mark important areas for intensive probing
Think through situations—evaluate
Ask—"who, when, what, how, where"
Allow the Scriptures to be the problem-solver

Be Hopeful
There are answers. God is the God of solutions.
The Bible is the textbook on counseling.
Model to show that victory is possible.
Label sin as sin. Take it seriously.
Don't use labels or terms that indicate defeat.
Don't be fooled or manipulated.
Remember that Christ is the greatest counselor.

Be Resourceful
Assign appropriate homework to problems.
Expect change through doing the homework.
Work on one problem at a time.
Clarify expectations—be simple and clear.
Homework will speed up level of changed behavior.
Dependence is established upon the power of the Holy Spirit.
Homework lets the progress be seen and measured and creates accountability to God and others.

Be Competent
Be—a Christian
Be—Spirit-filled
Be—Familiar with the Scriptures
Be—Capable of solving your own problems
Be—Empathetic
Be—Knowledgeable about personal relations
Be—A specialist in applied Christianity

"Biblical counseling in its fullest sense is simply an application of the means of sanctification." This means achieving Christlikeness through change. Christians must change in order to become more like Christ. "Counseling involves helping people to put off old patterns which grew out of rebellion toward God, and helping them to put on new practices which grow out of obedience to God."

Notes taken from Dr. Jay Adams Nouthetic Counseling Workshop, Faith Baptist Church, Lafayette, IN (1990).

John F. Gillette, Ph.D.

OUR DECISIONS

The lot is cast into the lap, but its every decision is from the LORD.

Proverbs 16:33

christian counseling teaching tools

Christian decision-making involves eight steps.

1. Confrontation: List some of the special situations in which you want to determine the will of God. What can you do to determine God's will?

Example: I want to know if God wants me to work with our children's ministries. I have been reading God's Word and waiting on him.

2. Confidence: What facts about God help give you comfort as you wait for God's will to be revealed?

Example: Proverbs 3:5–6: God will direct my paths. Psalm 23:1: I will not be in want.

3. Confession: What are the conditions for divine guidance?

Example: Psalm 32:5: Acknowledge my sin, confess it, and be forgiven. Romans 12:1–2: Renew my mind. 2 Timothy 3:16–17: Be familiar with Scripture in order to be equipped for good works.

4. Commandments: What are some areas where the Bible can provide guidance?

Example: 2 Corinthians 6:14 and 9:6–7: Be separate from evil, and I will reap what I sow. 1 Peter 2:15: Do good.

5. Communication: How can we know the will of God?

Example: Psalm 25:4–5: He will teach and guide me. Mark 11:24: Ask and believe. Ephesians 6:18–20: Pray with perseverance.

6. Council: What is wise for us to do to come to the will of God?

Example: Proverbs 12:15; 15:22; 20:18: Listen to advice, seek answers, make plans.

7. Commitment: What can we do to discern the will of God?

Example: Proverbs 16:3,9: Commit everything to God and make decisions based on God's word. 1 Corinthians 2:12,14: use the Spirit of God.

Confirmation: What questions should we ask before we make the final decisions? Here are some sample questions to ask yourself:

Am I running from a situation rather than patiently trusting God to work it out?
Psalm 11:1: Trust God.

Will my decision bring increased opportunities for Christian service?
2 Thessalonians 2:16—3:2: Service brings glory

Have I really prayed about the matter, and have I really desired to know and do God's will, no matter how much personal sacrifice is involved?

Have I seriously considered the outcome of my decision?

Will my decision bring reproach upon God, or will it glorify him?

Will my decision be for the good of God's people?

Do I have all the facts straight?

John F. Gillette, Ph.D.

DEPRESSION

Why are you downcast, O my soul?
Why so disturbed within me?
Put your hope in God,
for I will yet praise him,
my Savior and my God.

Psalm 43:5

christian counseling teaching tools

WHAT IS DEPRESSION?

"Remember that depression doesn't result directly from any one of several factors, but rather comes from a cyclical process in which the initial problem is mishandled in such a way that it is enlarged in downward helixical spirals that eventually plunge one into despair."

Depression is the downward slide of a person's life. It results from continued poor decision-making and choices. The downward cycle enslaves, but the reverse pattern, the biblical response, leads to a solution. This victory strengthens one's ability to solve new problems.

How can you reverse the downward spiral into despair? How can you find success in dealing with your emotions? Work through the following list of questions.

A Guide to Active, Positive Results

What is the initial problem? (Explore your inner thoughts.)

Make a list of patterns that determine failure or success.

When I do this: The result is: Failure/Success

Are you surrendering to your feelings rather than responding to them in light of your responsibilities as a Christian?

How is your response to humor or pleasant situations?

What are some feeling factors that increase depression for you?

What does God want you to do with your depression?

Some practical things you can do when you are depressed.

1. Expect pain. When it comes, evaluate it realistically. Write about it, your feelings, and your responses to it.

2. God is in control. Write down his attributes. Meditate on them.

3. Be honest: Do you dwell on failures and injustices? How can you retrain your thinking?

4. Don't isolate yourself. Challenge your thinking process by interacting with others.

5. Memorize Philippians 4:8 and make it part of your life.

Now that you have worked through this assignment, what do you want to see as the next step?

John F. Gillette, Ph.D.

OUR DESCRIPTION

> My sheep listen to my voice; I know them, and they follow me. I give them eternal life, and they shall never perish; no one can snatch them out of my hand.
>
> *John 10:27–28*

christian counseling teaching tools

Who are you?

If someone just met you yesterday, how would that person describe you? How would you friends describe you? What about your family? See, the closer we are to people, the more they know about us and the better they can describe us.

What would God say about you? How would he describe your relationship with him? Are the two of you close? How would you describe God? Do you know him well?

The way you are described by Jesus in John 10 is as a sheep—if you are a Christian. And Jesus describes himself as a shepherd. The bond between a sheep and its shepherd is unique. How do you think that relationship is similar to the way your relationship is to Christ?

If you look closely at John 10:27–28, you can see Christ's description of a Christian. How can you know you are a sheep?

"Listen to my voice"
Do you have sensitivity to the Word of God?

"I know them"
Do you have fellowship with Jesus?

"They follow me"
Are you obedient?

"I give them eternal life"
Do you know where your life will be spent?

"They shall never perish"
Do you have assurance in the Word?

"No one can snatch them out of my hand"
Do you have security in the Word?

The words of the following song reflect the longing to be like Jesus and become one of his followers.

> My one desire is to be like thee
> Cleanse me with thy love's pure fire
> May every precept thou hast taught me
> Into my daily life be wrought
> Lord, let me do thy will divine.
> Let each new dawn bring me more like thee.
> Grant me thy peace and keep me pure in heart and mind
> With strength to do each task assigned.
> This is my prayer I request.

What is your greatest desire?

How would you like others to describe you?

What would it take to become that person?

Now that you have worked through this assignment, what do you want to see as the next step?

John F. Gillette, Ph.D.

OUR ENABLEMENT

May the God of peace, who through the blood of the eternal covenant brought back from the dead our Lord Jesus, that great Shepherd of the sheep, equip you with everything good for doing his will, and may he work in us what is pleasing to him, through Jesus Christ, to whom be glory for ever and ever. Amen.

Hebrews 13:20–21

christian counseling teaching tools

Do you ever feel that you are unable to face a certain situation? Maybe you feel unable to influence a certain feeling or addiction. God wants you to have the power to live a victorious Christian life. What is holding you down? Think through areas in your life where you feel defeated. Ask God to show you areas to work on.

Now that you have identified some areas of concern, how do you tackle the part of your life that gives you the most discouragement? How do you gain victory? How are you given strength to carry out your Christian walk?

Let's examine the Scripture on page 1, and see how we might have the power we desire in our lives.

"May the God of peace"
Authority is found in our Creator-Redeemer. He is the author and dispenser of peace. We can trust our lives to him. Peace is the result of that trust.

"Blood of the eternal covenant"
The blood Christ shed on the cross secures God's promises for those who believe. We can rest on the decision of faith to rely on God's Word. His Word is power.

"Brought back from the dead"
Jesus is the focus of this phrase. He is life because he conquered death. Enablement is ours through the power of the resurrection. If you believe in Christ and his power, you have access to the power of God!

"Our Lord Jesus"
We can enjoy our life in Christ because Jesus is Lord. He is superior. He is master.

"Great Shepherd"
Christ accomplished all his saving work for us. We have no needs that he cannot meet. He will care for us better than anyone or anything.

"Equip you with everything good"
God will prepare us. He will make us fit. The promise is spiritual enablement. He will enable us for all we have to face.

"For doing his will, and may he work in us what is pleasing to him"
Our duty is to please God through our good work. Under the new covenant that God has with us through our belief in Christ, the power to do his will is given as he reveals his will. The key is to will our will to him. His will should be our desire.

"Through Jesus Christ"
The emphasis is not on receiving but on development. When we received salvation, we received all we needed. Now we must develop those gifts. It involves time, sacrifice, obedience, discipline, fellowship, and trust.

"To whom be glory for ever and ever"
Jesus Christ is the object of glory. We are invited to participate in God's plan to bring honor to our Savior. Our entire life here and hereafter is to honor, glorify, praise, and worship.

Amen

When God says "amen," it means "it is and shall be so." When we say "amen," it means "so let it be." God will keep his promises and enable us to be all he wants us to be. His purposes will be established. Let us focus our mind, heart and life on Christ.

Spend a few minutes thanking God for his power. Then use it!

John F. Gillette, Ph.D.

THE ENEMY

For, as I have often told you before and now say again even with tears, many live as enemies of the cross of Christ.

Philippians 3:18

christian counseling teaching tools

WHO IS OUR ENEMY?

The Christian's conflicts and trials are wholly accounted for within three realities—the flesh, the world, and the devil. The flesh is that nature that leads us to do wrong (Romans 7:21). The world is the realm of the devil, who seeks only evil for us (Ephesians 6:12).He is our enemy (1 Peter 5:8).

Let's look at the Scriptures and learn more about our enemy in order to defeat him:

Where did Satan come from?

God is the creator of all things, even spiritual beings (Colossians 1:15–18). As an anointed cherub, Lucifer became Satan when he tried to make himself, not only equal with God, but above God.

How did Satan fall?

Satan's sin is essentially the same as human sin. His five statements beginning with the words, "I will" detail his downfall (Isaiah 14:12–17). This once-mighty angel of God opposed the plan and purpose of God.

Read the following verses and answer the questions.

1. Does Satan work alone? Who works with him?

Matthew 25:41; Revelation 12:7–12

Daniel 10:12—11:1; Matthew 12:24–30; Ephesians 6:10–12

2. Are people exempt from his reign? John 8:44; 1 John 3:8–10

3. Is the church out of his area of attack? Revelation 2:9; 3:9

4. How does he deceive people? 2 Corinthians 4:4; 11:14

5. How does he try to hurt people? Mark 4:15; Luke 13:16; Acts 10:38; 2 Corinthians 12:7–8; Revelation 2:10

6. How does Satan influence our thoughts and actions? John 13:2 Acts 5:3; 1 Corinthians 7:5; 2 Timothy 2:26

The Bible tells us that Satan will be judged.

God will at some point in time completely defeat Satan and confine him and his allies to torment forever (Revelation 20:10). Christ has already defeated death and hell by providing salvation to all who believe in him (Acts 26:17–18). We don't need to fear Satan because Jesus has already won our battle for us (Hebrews 2:14; 1 John 3:8).

We do have a responsibility to fight against Satan while we are here on earth. What can we do to stand up to Satan? Read the following verses.

2 Corinthians 2:11

Ephesians 4:27

Ephesians 6:11–18

James 4:11

1 Peter 5:8–9

Now that you have worked through this assignment, what do you want to see as the next step?

John F. Gillette, Ph.D.

OUR FAITH

I am not ashamed of the gospel, because it is the power of God for the salvation of everyone who believes: first for the Jew, then for the Gentile. For in the gospel a righteousness from God is revealed, a righteousness that is by faith from first to last, just as it is written: "The righteous will live by faith."

Romans 1:16–17

christian counseling teaching tools

Faith is a gift from God, but what does it really mean to have faith?

The passage from Romans talks about faith "from first to last." How can we have that kind of faith in our lives?

Faith from first to last starts when we accept Jesus Christ as our Savior. When we believe that he is the Son of God, our faith is put into action. We believe that through his death and resurrection, we have life in him. But now God wants us to go further. He wants us to realize that not only is Christ in us and our lives in him, but Christ must live through us. That kind of faith is the faith that carries us to the end of our lives here on earth. Faith to the last.

WHERE DOES OUR FAITH COME FROM?

Read Ephesians 2:8–9. Where is our faith from?

Read Romans 5:1. What does faith do for us? Is this "first faith" or "last faith"?

Read Colossians 1:23. What is our responsibility when it comes to faith?

Read 1 Thessalonians 1:3. What does faith produce in your life?

Jesus said, "I have come that they may have life, and have it to the full" (John 10:10). Jesus wants us to have the kind of faith that leads to a full life—not just saving faith, although that is important—but faith for our everyday walk.

What does this faith look like? It is a faith that is imaginative, daring to expect the impossible. It is a faith that asks what God wants—not what we want. It is fearless faith! It is faith ready for anything.

This faith is the confidence that what God determines for our lives, he will also provide for, no matter what we face in our world.

This is a faith of patience, as we realize that God will work out our circumstances in his time. He is never too early or too late. He is always right on time.

This faith is an adventure, as we put our trust in God and risk our future by giving up control, knowing that it is the only way to assure our future.

Is this the kind of faith you have right now? What do you need to do to have this kind of faith?

Now that you have worked through this assignment, what do you want to see as the next step?

John F. Gillette, Ph.D.

FEAR

Have no fear of sudden disaster or of the ruin that overtakes the wicked, for the LORD will be your confidence and will keep your foot from being snared.

Proverbs 3:25–26

christian counseling teaching tools

WHAT IS FEAR?

Fear can mean different things. The Bible says, "Blessed are all who fear the LORD, who walk in his ways" (Psalm 128:1). In this verse, fear means "awe" or "reverence," especially toward God, the Supreme Being. The result of fear toward God will be trust and confidence in his care. When we fear God, we do not cringe before him. Instead, we are peaceful and secure. The Bible assures us: "My God will meet all your needs according to his glorious riches in Christ Jesus" (Philippians 4:19).

What about the other definition of fear?

The word *fear* can also refer to a painful emotion marked by dread or anxious concern. This type of fear about real or imagined situations can be debilitating for the person who experiences this emotion on a regular basis. Even for those for feel fear only occasionally, it can be an uncomfortable and unhappy experience.

Fear is an emotion that can disrupt your life and service to God and others.

What do the following verses say about fear and what our attitude should be toward the emotion of fear?

What does Jesus say about fear? Read Luke 12:4–7.

What does Paul say about fear? Read Romans 8:15–17.

What does Peter say about fear? Read 1 Peter 3:13–14.

What does John say about fear? Read 1 John 4:16–18.

In summary, how should we feel about fear? Read Hebrews 13:6 and 1 Peter 5:7.

Jesus told his followers: "Therefore do not worry about tomorrow, for tomorrow will worry about itself. Each day has enough trouble of its own" (Matthew 6:34). God gives us manageable portions of life—one day at a time. If our future were given to us all at once, we would be overwhelmed. So God broke up our lives into small portions which we can manage one day at a time. So forget the pain of yesterdays, do not worry about tomorrow, and deal with today.

> Life by the yard is hard.
> Life by the inch is a cinch.

So what to do with the yesterdays and tomorrows?

If you belong to God through Jesus Christ, he has all your yesterdays, and he forgives all that was amiss in them. He will also give you grace and power to face your anxieties for your tomorrows. God's grace is like manna. When it's kept over to the next day, it spoils. So asks for his help today, and then ask for it again tomorrow. Be encouraged. He takes all your fears one day at a time.

Now that you have worked through this assignment, what do you want to see as the next step?

John F. Gillette, Ph.D.

Feeling Inferior

Be self-controlled and alert. Your enemy the devil prowls around like a roaring lion looking for someone to devour. Resist him, standing firm in the faith, because you know that your brothers throughout the world are undergoing the same kind of sufferings.

1 Peter 5:8

christian counseling teaching tools

What is a Feeling of Inferiority?

Feeling inferior involves a sense of inadequacy. It is a weapon that Satan uses to weaken our usefulness. He knows how to exploit our weaknesses to bring about discouragement, disappointment, and failure. A feeling of inferiority leads to all these feelings and more.

What is the result of feeling inferior?

A feeling of inferiority will paralyze our human potential.
　　　When we feel inferior, we are often afraid to use our gifts. We don't believe that our contributions are important.

A feeling of inferiority will destroy our dreams.
　　　When we feel inferior, we lose our vision of what we can do through God's help.

A feeling of inferiority will ruin our relationships.
　　　When we feel inferior, our perceptions become contaminated. We don't see how our relationships really are.

A feeling of inferiority will take away any useful service we might do.
　　　When we feel inferior, we focus on our infirmities and cease to try to help others.

WHO ARE YOU?

We decide who we are from our earliest system of relationships, by how we were treated and loved as we were growing up. No matter what relationships you experienced here on earth, your Father in heaven has known you for a long time.

What does Psalm 139:13–16 say about your earliest relationship to God?

We decide who we are through the physical, emotional, and intellectual equipment we bring into the world. No matter who we are, what we look like, or how smart we are, God has a relationship with us.

What does Colossians 1:26–29 say about God's love for all people?

We decide who we are through our understanding of our spiritual state. Beginning with the first sin of Adam and Eve, a chain reaction of imperfect parenting was set in motion. Our parents failed to raise us perfectly through ignorance, misguided actions, and conditional love. As a result, we are damaged by their failures.

What does Matthew 7:11 say about our perfect heavenly Father?

Feelings of inferiority result from various relationships and situations, but our main way of determining who we are will benefit us if we define ourselves through our relationship with God.

You belong to God, have worth and competence because you are loved and held up by the sovereign, almighty God who accepts you as you are. He has given you unique abilities and gifts (1 Corinthians 12:4–6). He has made you into a new creature (2 Corinthians 5:17). He has forgiven all your sins (1 John 1:9). God has given you a real reason for self-esteem.

You are a whole person when you stand with God. Your feelings of inferiority can be a stepping stone, not a stumbling block, to spiritual maturity.

Now that you have worked through this assignment, what do you want to see as the next step?

John F. Gillette, Ph.D.

OUR FEELINGS

But the Counselor, the Holy Spirit, whom the Father will send in my name, will teach you all things and will remind you of everything I have said to you.

John 14:26

christian counseling teaching tools

ARE FEELINGS EVER "WRONG"?

Our feelings are important. We cannot neglect their influence in our lives. Feelings are neither right nor wrong; they are simply there. They are vital and necessary in our make-up as human beings. What we do with our feelings makes them right or wrong. So as we seek to understand them, to identify them and deal with them effectively, we will grow to appreciate all our feelings.

How are we to know how to deal with our many different feelings?

The Bible is always the text book that we need to find out if something is right or wrong. It is the book of principles, policies, and practices that we are given by God.

Let's examine some Scriptures that will help us determine what to do with our feelings.

Read the following verses and meditate on the truths found there.

- Isaiah 41:10. God will help us!
- Proverbs 18:10. Emotions may feel unsafe, but God is safety.
- Philippians 4:13. We don't have to worry about feelings overcoming us. We have strength through Christ.
- 2 Corinthians 12:9. We can rejoice that God will care for us. We don't have to worry about being weak.

You can boldly claim God's strength for every challenge and opportunity in daily life. God tells us that he can do anything. If we ask him, he will give us the strength to face anything.

How does this strength develop?

Our inner spiritual strength develops as we allow the Spirit to work in our lives. Moment by moment, day by day, the fruit of that faith will be seen. As we handle our feelings correctly through the Scriptural standards, we will find God's strength, which will then produce competence in our lives. That competence is built through our relationship with God and the Holy Spirit.

Read the following Scriptures and write down what you learn about the Holy Spirit.
John 14:17

John 14:26

Romans 8:14

Romans 8:26–27

Galatians 5:22–23

The Christian life was meant to be lived only in the power of the Holy Spirit. We need to allow the Holy Spirit to fill us and empower us. This filling does not come from without but from within. From the point that we received Christ, the Holy Spirit has indwelt us. But we need to continually ask God to fill us with the Spirit, to empower the Spirit to guide our thought and decisions—and emotions.

If we are going to handle our feelings properly, we must hunger and thirst for righteousness (Matthew 5:6). We must surrender our will to Christ (Romans 12:1). We must confess every known sin and accept his cleansing and forgiveness (1 John 1:9).

Thank God right now for the Holy Spirit in you.

Now that you have worked through this assignment, what do you want to see as the next step?

John F. Gillette, Ph.D.

OUR GIFTS

Each one should use whatever gift he has received to serve others, faithfully administering God's grace in its various forms.

1 Peter 4:10

christian counseling teaching tools

WHAT ARE SPIRITUAL GIFTS?

The body of Christ, which is the church, is composed of many different people with many different strengths and abilities (1 Corinthians 12:12–13). Each member is given a special gift or gifts from God through the Holy Spirit for the benefit of the church (1 Corinthians 12:27–31).

Do I have a spiritual gift?

If you are a Christian, you have a spiritual gift.

How do I know what it is?

God will reveal your gift to you fi you ask in faith. On the next page is a chart showing some spiritual gifts.

Read through the following chart and identify gifts you may have.

Gifts	Meaning	Scripture
Administration	Governor, organize, superintend, delegate	1 Corinthians 12:28
Leadership	Leading and caring actively with zeal	Romans 12:8; 1 Timothy 3:1–5
Evangelism	Communication of the Good News—one to one witnessing	Acts 21:8; Ephesians 4:11
Exhortation	Encourage, counsel, urge, beseech, give explicit advice	Romans 12:8
Prophecy	Speak forth, up-build, encourage, console, preach, explain, apply	1 Corinthians 14:1
Knowledge	Spiritually mature, intelligent judgement, studious	1 Corinthians 2:11–16; 12:8
Wisdom	Interpret truth, produce solutions to problems, apply knowledge to spiritual life—consistent insight, respected opinion	1 Corinthians 12:8; Proverbs 1:5
Pastoring	Protective care, equip others to serve Christ by serving each other—help release potential in the flock	John 21:16; Ephesians 4:11
Teaching	Explain God's truth and apply it	Romans 12:7; 1 Corinthians 12:28–29
Faith	Wonder-work, utter dependence, visionary	1 Corinthians 12:9; 13:1–3
Giving	Sharing, imparting, eager to give without benefit	Matthew 6:3–4; Romans 12:8
Ministering	Any area that supports someone else	Romans 12:7
Discernment	Judge—evaluate intuitively, natural, spiritual, gifted watchmen	1 Corinthians 12:10
Mercy	Sympathize, personal care, cheerful	Romans 12:8
Hospitality	Welcome guests, willing spirit	1 Peter 4:9

You may have one gift or a few gifts. God will reveal your gifts to you if you ask.

After reviewing the list of gifts, write down 3 or 4 you think you might have. Then look in the Bible to see what God has to say about such gifts. Read the Scriptures references. You might want to look in a Bible concordance to find other examples of the gifts at work.

Also, ask a few close Christian friends what gifts they see manifested in you.

And continue to pray. God will reveal your gifts to you.

John F. Gillette, Ph.D.

OUR GOD

He is the image of the invisible God, the firstborn over all creation.

Colossians 1:15

christian counseling teaching tools

WHO IS CHRIST?

One of the facts of the human mind is that a person only thinks as much as he or she has to. But it is important for us to concentrate our God-given abilities on thinking through the facts and things we know to be true.

So who is Christ? Who is our God?

Think through those questions, then turn to the next page.

WHO IS CHRIST?

Colossians 1:15 calls Christ the "image of the invisible God." What is an image?

Read Genesis 1:27. People were created in God's image. How do you think people are an image of God?

What does it mean to be "firstborn"? Read Genesis 4:4. Why is it significant that the fat of the firstborn was offered?

So how do these concepts relate to Christ? Read Hebrews 1:1–3. How is Christ the image of God?

Read Hebrews 1:6. Why is it important that we know Christ is the firstborn of God?

WHO IS CHRIST?

The human soul is dark until it is enlightened by Christ.

> All things have been committed to me by my Father. No one knows the Son except the Father, and no one knows the Father except the Son and those to whom the Son chooses to reveal him. "Come to me, all you who are weary and burdened, and I will give you rest. Take my yoke upon you and learn from me, for I am gentle and humble in heart, and you will find rest for your souls. For my yoke is easy and my burden is light."
> Matthew 11:27–28.

Christ is able to meet all our needs because he is God!

John F. Gillette, Ph.D.

THE GOSPEL

I want to remind you of the gospel . . . that Christ died for
our sins according to the Scriptures, that he was buried,
that he was raised on the third day according to the
Scriptures.

1 Corinthians 15:1,3–4

christian counseling teaching tools

What is the Gospel?

The *gospel* is word that means "Good News." And the Good News is the message found in the Bible, that Jesus Christ died for our sins and rose again. He did this to provide salvation for all who ask and believe in him. Let's look at the Scriptures and see that Good News in detail:

"According to the Scriptures"
The Scriptures refer to God's Word, the Bible. Through careful study of the evidence, we can have confidence that the Bible is God's Word.

"Christ died"
God, the supernatural being who created the heavens and the earth, loved us and gave his Son to die for us. Jesus Christ, the Son of God, became our substitute for the penalty of sin.

"For our sins"
Sin refers to rebellion against God. It is disobedience. It is not measuring up to his standards. We have inherited sinful nature through the disobedience of the first people, Adam and Eve, back in the garden of Eden.

The only way to accepted by God and have sin erased is through believing that Christ carried our sins to the grave and experienced the punishment that we deserved. We have been forgiven and set free by God when we believe that he died for us.

"That he was raised on the third day"
The issue of sin has been taken care of through Christ's death. Through Christ's resurrection, the believer then has the power to do what God wants. Through our belief in Christ we have been given a new nature. But we must chose to believe. It is a deliberate choice and practice, not something automatic.

JESUS IS THE WAY!

The gospel is Good News because it makes new people of those who believe. We can't change on our own. Through Christ, God changes us into people that are more like him.

If you have a problem with the authority of the Bible, study it.

1. Who loves us? John 3:16

2. Who is the way? John 14:6

3. Who has sinned? Romans 3:23

4. What is the penalty for sin? Romans 6:23

5. How are we saved? Acts 16:31

Have you ever prayed this prayer?

> Dear God,
> I know that I am a sinner. I believe that you love me and that you sent your Son to die on the cross to pay the penalty for my sin. I believe in you and trust you completely. Come into my heart and control my live. Thank you, Lord.

Faith is primarily a decision to trust ourselves to something or someone. We have learned the facts concerning sin. We are sinful, and we must make a personal response to God in order to have a relationship with him. "I have to make a decision to believe what God has to say and to trust Jesus Christ as my only hope of forgiveness and eternal life."

Have you prayed the prayer to trust in Jesus? If so, what assurance do you have of your salvation decision? Read John 1:12

Now that you have worked through this assignment, what do you want to see as the next step?

John F. Gillette, Ph.D.

OUR GUIDE

Therefore, my dear friends, as you have always obeyed—not only in my presence, but now much more in my absence—continue to work out your salvation with fear and trembling, for it is God who works in you to will and to act according to his good purpose.

Philippians 2:12–13

christian counseling teaching tools

WHAT SHOULD BE OUR CODE OF CONDUCT AND HOW SHOULD WE FIND IT?

We know that God's Word contains a guide for our lives. Do we read it on a regular basis? And do we put the words into action in our lives? Obedience to God's teachings is a good start, but a code of conduct goes beyond obedience.

The writer of Psalm 101 says, "I will be careful to lead a blameless life" (verse 2). Of course, we cannot lead a blameless life in our own power. We can turn to God's power to find the way to a blameless life. Look at the following page for steps to developing a code of conduct that will lead to a blameless life.

Conversion

Turn away from sin, and turn to God. Read Luke 24:46–47. How will the preaching of Christ accomplish this? How does this teaching affect your own life?

Consecration

Be dedicated to God. Read Romans 12:1–2. Why is it necessary to have Jesus as Lord of your life?

Conscience

Have an inner judge of moral issues. Read Romans 2:14–15. How does knowing you have a inner conscience affect your life?

Confirmation

Be assured of righteousness. Read 1 John 2:29. Others watch us to see if we "do righteousness." If you live in Christ, you will bear the same fruit that Christ bore. What kind of fruit are you bearing in your life?

Commission

You have a special assignment. Read Matthew 28:19–20. You have a calling to be active in God's work, the church. True success lies in following God's call. What work are you doing for Christ?

What kind of code guides your conduct right now?

Pray and ask God to show you his will for you. Ask him to show you where you are lacking in obedience and for help to follow him more fully.

God will guide your conduct through his Word.

What will you begin to read from God's Word that will shape your conduct?

Now that you have worked through this assignment, what do you want to see as the next step?

John F. Gillette, Ph.D.

OUR IMPOSSIBILITIES

Do not be afraid. Stand firm and you will see the deliverance the LORD will bring you today.

Exodus 14:13

christian counseling teaching tools

What is "impossible" in your life?

Where have you given up in defeat?

The Scripture from Exodus is what Moses said to the Israelites as they faced their enemies, the Egyptians. They had made their exodus from Egypt, but now great armies from Pharaoh, king of Egypt, are in hot pursuit. The Israelites are now on the shoreline of a large body of water. There is no where to go. They cannot turn back, and they cannot go forward—north, south, east, west—all routes of escape are closed.

What Moses and the people need to do is look up. From that direction will come hope for escape. God will give Moses and his people what they need to succeed.

Let's examine Exodus 14:13.

"Do not be afraid"
How do we rid ourselves of fear? We need to trust God. He is within us and is in charge of all our impossibilities. Sometimes God allows struggles in our lives so that we will grow on our spiritual walk with him and therefore bring glory to him. We are able to change our emotion of fear when we trust in God and realize who he really is— the author and creator of all things and the universal ruler. We can trust him.

What are you afraid of? How can you trust God with your fear?

"Stand firm"
This means what it says: Take a stand. Fear makes us run in all different directions to escape from the real or perceived threat. What we must do is remember the promises that he has given us and the victories he has given us.

Read the following promises from God:
- Psalm 31:24
- 1 Corinthians 10:13
- 2 Thessalonians 3:3

What are some past victories that you can remember?

"See the deliverance [of] the Lord"
Expect God to work. Each miracle God performs in our lives is preparation for greater trust in the future. The only things that can hurt us are things we refuse to turn over to God.

Verse 13 in Exodus 14 is followed by another command from Moses. He tells the people, "The LORD will fight for you; you need only to be still" (verse 14).

There is a time to keep still before God. Once you have prayed and shown him your fear, keep still. Listen. Observe God working in your life.

The rest of Exodus 14 tells the result of the story of Moses and the Israelites. All seemed hopeless, but Moses trusted God. And God made a way through the water for Moses and the people. And the Egyptian army was destroyed.

God's guidance and power will never be ahead of time. It will never be late. It will always come at the right time. Give God whatever impossible situation you face. He will take care of it.

Now that you have worked through this assignment, what do you want to see as the next step?

John F. Gillette, Ph.D.

OUR MIND

Be transformed by the renewing of your mind.

Romans 12:2

christian counseling teaching tools

In Romans 12:1, Paul says, "I urge you." He is urging his readers to listen, to respond, and accept the gift of God. What is this gift? We can receive a new electro-chemical computer (brain/mind).

Long ago, people thought that the mind was an invisible inner representative of self and could be understood only by looking beyond humans for an explanation. The Greeks thought that the mind was a function of the body and that behavior was a product of the mind. Today, we have many views of the mind, and many different areas of study relate to the mind.

> The mind and philosophy involve speculation.
> The mind and physiology involve observation.
> The mind and physics involve measurement.
> The mind and psychology involve testing.
> The mind and theology involve reconstruction.

The last area is the one I would like for us to focus upon. We control our brain, thinking, and emotions. We are directly responsible for our actions. We choose how we think and feel. Difficulties are, for the most part, self-induced, maintained, magnified, and distorted.

We can be free from anxiety, doubts, fears, uncertainty, and worry. We can be free from anger, depression, envy, guilt, hatred, hostility, and jealousy. It all depends on what we put our faith in. Faith requires initiation, action, and commitment. All of this takes place in our minds. Everything we do ultimately is the result of our thoughts.

What Kind of Mind Do You Have?

The Depraved Mind
See Romans 1:28–32. This mind rejects God. It puts God out of its thoughts and leads to a lifestyle of open defiance toward God.

The Blinded Mind
See 2 Corinthians 4:3–4. This mind is unwilling to accept God. It can be face to face with miracles and not believe.

The Defiled Mind
See Mark 7:20–23. This mind is one that is unclean. Evil thoughts generated in a heart united with evil will produce evil words and actions. The source is from inside one's heart.

The Vain Mind
See Ephesians 4:17–19. This mind is wasting its time, for it is unproductive. It is insensitive to the truth and concerned with greed and selfishness. It is void of useful aims and goals.

The Doubtful Mind
See James 1:5–8. The doubtful mind is one that is confused and frustrated. It is unsteady, staggering, uncertain, and mixed up.

The Carnal Mind
See Romans 8:5–8. The carnal mind is the mind of the world. It is not pleasing to God. It is concerned with temporal and material matters.

The Renewed Mind
See 1 John 3:23–24. This mind is a reflection of God's love. It is a mind of confidence in the name of Christ, which is undergirded by love. It is a mind of obedience to God's commands in faith and love. It is the verification that God lives in this mind by the operation of God's Spirit in the life.

HOW CAN YOU GET CONTROL OF YOUR MIND?

Power is possible to those who have faith, hope, trust, and belief. It is for those who can visualize success and victory.

Renew your electro-chemical computer!

God has shown us that our minds are battlegrounds between forces of good and evil. He has also shown us how we can successfully choose life or death. The renewed mind is gift from God to all who believe in and follow Jesus Christ as the Son of God.

We only act on the thoughts we believe. Please believe that:

> God so loved the world that he gave his one and only Son, that whoever believes in him shall not perish but have eternal life (John 3:16).

Only when we truly make Jesus a part of ourselves will we receive his power.

He came to that which was his own, but his own did not receive him. Yet to all who received him, to those who believed in his name, he gave the right to become children of God (John 1:11–12).

John F. Gillette, Ph.D.

OUR PERSONAL DEVELOPMENT

And we pray this in order that you may live a life worthy of the Lord and may please him in every way: bearing fruit in every good work, growing in the knowledge of God, being strengthened with all power according to his glorious might so that you may have great endurance and patience, and joyfully giving thanks to the Father, who has qualified you to share in the inheritance of the saints in the kingdom of light.

Colossians 1:10–12

christian counseling teaching tools

Dedication to development moves us from the finite to the infinite while we are still living in a mortal body.

Take a minute to evaluate your current state of spiritual development.

- Knowing that Jesus Christ is in you will be the sure foundation for limitless building.
Read 2 Corinthians 13:5 and Romans 10:9. Are you sure of your personal salvation?

- Consecration involves becoming a participant, not an observer.
Read Romans 12:1–2. Is your life consecrated to Christ?

- A thorough working knowledge of the Bible is necessary. Filling your head with knowledge without filling your heart will bring only emptiness.
Read 2 Timothy 2:15. Are you learning the Word?

- Just think! We have a private line from God's heart to ours.
Read John 16:24 and Hebrews 10:19–22; 4:15–16. Are you praying?

- The fruit of the Spirit (Galatians 5:22–23) will be characterized in our lives if we obey God's Word.
Read 2 Corinthians 9:13. Are you obedient?

- Become men and women of destiny.
Read Romans 10:17 and Hebrews 11:6. Are you expanding your faith?

- Growth comes in intermediate, successive steps that move to the impossible.

Read Ephesians 1:17. Are you exercising wisdom and common sense?

- Discover the gift that can best serve Christ. Then serve the church with it.

Read 2 Timothy 1:6. Are you developing your gift(s)?

- The message of the gospel is clear and changeless. How can we bring the gospel with renewed impact to our changing generation?

Read Hebrews 13:8. Are you cultivating creativity?

- The only thing any of us really have in this passing world is the moment that is now . . . present. Don't waste today with regrets of yesterday or daydreams of tomorrow.

Read Ephesians 5:16. Is your time used properly?

- No Christian should be ineloquent in expressing the gospel of Christ.

Read 1 Corinthians 14:1. Are you communicating clearly?

- Reliability proves that the spiritual walk is meaningful.

Read 1 Corinthians 15:58. Are you steadfast for Christ?

After reading through the Scriptures and questions, what do you evaluate as your own state of personal development? Ask yourself where you are. Ask God to help you determine where you need to develop.

Below, write out three areas you could concentrate on developing further. Then write out a prayer to God for guidance and direction.

1.

2.

3.

Prayer:

Now that you have worked through this assignment, what do you want to see as the next step?

John F. Gillette, Ph.D.

Our Christian Philosophy

For from him and through him and to him are all things.
To him be the glory forever!

Romans 11:36

christian counseling teaching tools

How do we educate ourselves as Christians?

Christian education is based upon the Scripture. Its philosophy is based upon the Bible. It emphasizes a view that seeks to formulate a unified concept of God and his Word in the creation and nature of humanity.

Integration is the key to developing a coherent view of God. Think of a basket as an example of integration. If you were to take pieces of straw, they would not be a basket. But if you wove the straw together, you could end up with a finished product. The straw woven together makes a whole basket. In the same way, when you integrate many different ways of knowing about God—books, magazines, environment, friends, teachers—you can develop with a coherent view of God.

You have to choose from all the different influences and voices that tell you what to believe. You have to integrate all the information—weed out what you don't want and accept what is true. How can you go about making good choices? How can you share your philosophy to help others?

How can you develop a Christian philosophy?

One key element is **wisdom**:
Read Proverbs 4:7. What does the writer think about wisdom?

"Wisdom sees the integrity of the Divine Plan; by its light the truly wise man sees—at least in broad outline—the relationship of one truth to another, the beginning and the end of creation, one principle to another."

Read Proverbs 2:6. Where does wisdom originate?

The next key is **prudence**.
Read Proverbs 2:11. What does prudence mean to you? How can it be seen in your life?

The next key is **piety**.

Read Isaiah 6:3. Piety refers to a sentiment of love and respect for God. How does our knowledge of the character of God influence our love for him?

The final key is **activity**.
If wisdom reveals a person's destination, and prudence and piety chart the course, zeal is the steam of life that starts the engine. See Romans 12:11.

In order to determine a Christian philosophy for yourself, you must determine the truth based on your knowledge and experiences. And the Bible holds the principles for that knowledge.

If you have determined a Christian philosophy for yourself, you will be better able to share your convictions with others.

So what do you believe? Write out your own Christian philosophy below. Be ready to share it with others.

John F. Gillette, Ph.D.

OUR PRAISE

Praise the LORD.
Praise the LORD, O my soul.

Psalm 146:1

christian counseling teaching tools

ARE WE SUPPOSED TO PRAISE GOD?

The word Hallelujah occurs four times in the book of Revelation. The words *praise the Lord* appear forty-four times in the book of Psalms. We are witnessing rejoicing in such cases! In the Psalms it is the praise of earth, and in Revelation it is the praise of heaven. But in both cases, it is praise to God.

If we follow the Word of God, then we are to praise God!

Do you regularly praise God? If so, what do you praise him for?

Do you find it difficult to praise God? Do you wish you praised him more?

What can help you praise God more often?

Open your Bible to Psalm 105. This psalm deals with the history of Israel. The psalmist sees the footprints of God in history and in nature. Let's look at this praise psalm.

Read verses 9 and 10. What did God do for the patriarchs?

Read verses 12–15. What did God do for his people when they were wandering without a home?

Read verses 16–23. What did God do for the people through Joseph?

Read verses 24–37. How did God rescue his people?

Read verses 39–41. How did God care for his people?

Read verse 45. What does the psalmist say in response to God's actions for his people?

Have you ever thought about how you got to where you are now? Are you in a difficult situation now? Does it seem difficult to praise God? Write out what God has done in your life in the past.

What did God do for your parents?

What did God do for you as a child?

How did God bring you to salvation?

How did God work to bring you in contact with someone to counsel you?

Who has God placed in your life that has been a blessing to you?

What miracles have you seen in your life?

What is your response to what God has done for you?

Now that you have worked through this assignment, what do you want to see as the next step?

John F. Gillette, Ph.D.

OUR PROMISES

May the God of peace, who through the blood of the eternal covenant brought back from the dead our Lord Jesus, that great Shepherd of the sheep, equip you with everything good for doing his will, and may he work in us what is pleasing to him, through Jesus Christ, to whom be glory for ever and ever. Amen.

Hebrews 13:20–21

christian counseling teaching tools

How can we know the promises of God?

God's Word is a gift to us from him. What is in his Word? Do you know?

In God's Word are found many promises for us. Although the Bible was written many years ago, the promises in it are still valid for our lives today.

Jesus Christ is called our "shepherd," and we are called "sheep." People need spiritual, moral, and personal deliverance. Our shepherd has paved the way for such deliverance. He knows the location of the pasture, where to find water, food, and shade.

Because of Christ's death and resurrection, we now have a relationship with our shepherd. We can have peace and rest in our lives because of the work of Christ.

Read the following promises from the Word of God.

Read John 3:16 and Ephesians 1:7. Do you have a relationship with Christ?

Read Romans 15:4. What can the Word of God do for you in your present circumstances?

Read 1 John 1:4. How do you respond to the Word of God?

Read Proverbs 3:1–2. In what area of your life do you need peace?

We have security through our relationship with Christ and the promises of the Word of God. We know that God wants the best for us. He wants us to glorify him in all we do.

Set your priorities to follow after Christ.

What circumstances do you need guidance for?

What promises can you find in the Bible to apply to your situation?

How can you claim those promises for your life? What will you do to react differently to your circumstances?

Now that you have worked through this assignment, what do you want to see as the next step?

John F. Gillette, Ph.D.

OUR POWER

You do not have, because you do not ask God. When you ask, you do not receive, because you ask with wrong motives.

James 4:2–3

christian counseling teaching tools

What is Prayer?

Praying is serious business. When you pray, you are talking to God. When you read the Bible, God is talking to you. Have you ever wondered, "Why do I have so little victory over sin? Why does it seem I have no answers to my prayers?"

The power of prayer doesn't lie in a magic formula or in some act you can do. God wants to have a relationship with you. He just wants you to talk to him.

Prayer is simply talking to God.

There is no reason why you can't experience power in your daily life through prayer. It all begins with believing the words of the Bible.

Read Jeremiah 29:13. What does this verse tell you about prayer?

Read John 14:6. What is Christ's role in our prayers?

Read James 5:16. What type of person is in good communication with God?

Before you can take part in the power of prayer, you must first answer the question asked in Acts 16:30, "What must I do to be saved?" Have you answered that question already? If not, the answer is found in the next verse: "Believe in the Lord Jesus, and you will be saved" (verse 31).

Christ suffered and died to solve our problem of sin. He "died for our sins" (1 Corinthians 15:3) and "he died to sin" (Romans 6:10). When a person believes in Christ, he or she has participated in Christ's crucifixion, death, burial, and resurrection (Romans 6:1–10). Because of Christ, we can now have victory over sin every day.

Where does power in prayer come from?

Power comes from belief.

All people have sinned. We cannot measure up to God's standards on our own merits (Romans 3:23).

The result of sin is death. We deserve the penalty for sin, which is separation from God (Romans 6:23).

Christ died for us. We must receive God's remedy for sin and death (Romans 5:8).

If you call on his name, you'll be saved. When we believe, power comes into our lives (Romans 10:13).

How do you want to respond to this truth?

Now that you have worked through this assignment, what do you want to see as the next step?

John F. Gillette, Ph.D.

OUR RESPONSIBILITY

Do not conform any longer to the pattern of this world, but be transformed by the renewing of your mind. Then you will be able to test and approve what God's will is—his good, pleasing and perfect will.

Romans 12:2

christian counseling teaching tools

What has most influenced your life and actions? Do you sometimes feel a victim of your past? If so, then think about re-educating yourself.

"Christian Re-Educative Self-Counseling"

Our minds need to be re-educated. Whatever we have learned, we can also unlearn, relearn, or change through the re-education process. We must accept responsibility for our thinking, feelings, and behavior. We must reject the theory that we are wholly determined by our past. Our mental lives need to be based on reason, and our spiritual lives need to be based on faith. An objective analysis of our perceptions, thinking, feeling and behavior lends itself to three areas:
- Facts and events (our perceptions)
- Self-talk (our thoughts, attitudes, and beliefs in relation to the facts and events)
- Emotive feelings.

So get the facts, be objective, and choose the feeling you really want to experience.

Most of us operate more on feelings than on reason. Our minds are filled with memories, rational and irrational beliefs, ideas, attitudes, prejudices, biases, and fantasies. Everything within our minds must be evaluated with objective thinking. Only then can we determine what is true and how we are to act.

What does the Bible say about our thoughts and feelings?

Read 2 Corinthians 4:8. Do you have a choice over your feelings? What does this passage tell you about feelings?

Read 1 John 4:1–2. How can you determine what are positive thoughts?

What do you put into your mind regularly?

Read 2 Corinthians 10:4–5. How do you have victory in your thought life? Where does your power come from?

Read Proverbs 4:23. How can you guard your heart?

If we fill our lives with the wonder of Christ and the desire to be like him, our lives will change for the better. If we are ready with verses of Scripture in our minds, we will always be ready to combat Satan's lies with the truth of God's Word.

God lets us struggle so that in the end we will have a greater appreciation of him. Don't run from him when you fail or are in pain—run to him. He's waiting for you to fully surrender your heart to him.

What kind of relationship do you have with God?

We can reprogram our minds with God's Word. His Word will increase your faith and give you power to overcome negative thoughts. Try spending 20 minutes with God each day. It will keep you spiritually refreshed and keep your commitment to God firm.

We have problems dealing with our thoughts and feelings because we have made God fit our thinking, ideologies, dogmas, churches, or customs. We try to interpret him from our own limited knowledge and experience. If we focus on concentrating our thoughts on God and his Word, we will have success. Jesus tells us to pray and work, to have faith and reason, to hear and do. James 1:22 says, "Do not merely listen to the word, and so deceive yourselves. Do what it says."

Now that you have worked through this assignment, what do you want to see as the next step?

John F. Gillette, Ph.D.

OUR REWARD

Rejoice and be glad, because great is your reward in heaven.

Matthew 5:12

christian counseling teaching tools

Would you like to win a crown?

God is a rewarder of those who diligently seek him. First Corinthians 2:9 says, "No eye has seen, no ear has heard, no mind has conceived what God has prepared for those who love him."

Do you do things because of what you'll get? Or do you act with no motivation except to do good? Your heart attitude determines your success as a Christian. Do God's will because you want to please him, but also be glad! You will receive a reward for your service.

Have you ever wondered what kind of reward you'll receive?

The Crown is a Crown of Rejoicing

Philippians 4:1
Therefore, my brothers, you whom I love and long for, my joy and crown, that is how you should stand firm in the Lord, dear friends!

The Crown is a Crown of Righteousness

2 Timothy 4:6–8
For I am already being poured out like a drink offering, and the time has come for my departure. I have fought the good fight, I have finished the race, I have kept the faith. Now there is in store for me the crown of righteousness, which the Lord, the righteous Judge, will award to me on that day—and not only to me, but also to all who have longed for his appearing.

The Crown is a Crown of Glory

1 Peter 5:2–4
Be shepherds of God's flock that is under your care, serving as overseers—not because you must, but because you are willing, as God wants you to be; not greedy for money, but eager to serve; not lording it over those entrusted to you, but being examples to the flock. And when the Chief Shepherd appears, you will receive the crown of glory that will never fade away.

The Crown is a Crown of Life

James 1:12
Blessed is the man who perseveres under trial, because when he has stood the test, he will receive the crown of life that God has promised to those who love him.

Colossians 3:23–24:
Whatever you do, work at it with all your heart, as working for the Lord, not for men, since you know that you will receive an inheritance from the Lord as a reward. It is the Lord Christ you are serving.

God will reward your work. How are you serving him?

Pray the following prayer as a response of thanks.

God,
Help me to serve you. Help me to follow you. Help me to focus my eyes and thoughts on doing your will. Help me to seek the eternal, glorious rewards that you offer, not the temporary rewards of this life. Thank you for your abundant rewards.
In Jesus' name, amen.

John F. Gillette, Ph.D.

SATAN

"he is a liar"

John 8:44

christian counseling teaching tools

The symptoms of demon possession are subtle.
- Dishonesty gives Satan an entrance into our lives.
- Fear can also provide an entry.
- Satan exploits our negative feelings.
- We are victimized by rejection.
- Satan can take a foothold when we focus on the pain of the past.
- The sins of our ancestors are sometimes passed down in a family.
- Dabbling in the occult can give Satan an entrance.

The oppression of Satan can be discerned. What are some signs?

1. Satan takes the sins of the flesh and strengthens their power. What are some sins of the flesh evident in your life?

2. Satan reinforces the evil already in the human heart. Make a list of your sinful thoughts.

3. Once Satan gains a foothold, the victim feels powerless as destructive behavior is repeated. Have you allowed Satan a foothold in any area of your life? If so, where?

4. If you are preoccupied with destructive habits and unable to find a way out, obsession has taken place. Do you have compulsive behaviors? What are they?

5. Demonic spirits can invade the human body. Do you feel the presence of evil spirits?

The defeat of Satan can be assured.

Understand that Satan is the father of lies (John 8:44). He makes us question our value. He casts doubt on what we know is true. He exploits guilt and shame. He tries to make us believe that God does not have our best interest at heart. He tries to make it appear that God can't cleanse us or help us.

Has Satan deceived you? In what area? Admit your deception.

Submit to God. Repent of the sin that gives Satan his foothold. Renounce the sins, memories, and strongholds. Be truthful with God and yourself.

Accept Christ's authority. Is there any doubt that Christ has totally defeated Satan? Admit your doubts and ask God's forgiveness.

Confront the enemy with the word of God. Have you expelled thoughts from Satan and his influence? Use the Scripture to help you. Memorize the following verses. Make a goal to try to memorize a verse each week.

John 8:32
James 4:6–8
Colossians 2:15
Matthew 4:1–11
James 5:16
Romans 6:1–14

Pray in God's will through Christ's name and with the guidance of the Holy Spirit!

Pray for forgiveness.

Pray for strength.

Pray for wisdom.

Pray for discernment.

Pray for victory.

Now that you have worked through this assignment, what do you want to see as the next step?

John F. Gillette, Ph.D.

OUR SIN

Surely I was sinful at birth,
sinful from the time my mother conceived me.

Psalm 51:5

christian counseling teaching tools

AM I SINFUL?

The Bible tells us that all people are sinful. That's probably not what you wanted to hear!

In our culture, the word *sin* is not often used. People don't like to think of themselves as sinful. And people don't like to label others as sinful.

But in reality, sin is a disease that infects the entire human race. No group of people is exempt from sin. At the heart of all the troubles in the world lies sin.

Where does this sin come from?

If we examine the first book of the Bible, Genesis, we see right away that sin entered God's perfect world of creation through the deception of Satan (see Genesis 3). Satan is the enemy of God and therefore the enemy of all humans.

Read John 8:44. What did Jesus say about Satan?

Read Genesis 3:1–7. The serpent in this story is the devil, Satan, in disguise. When the first people had to make a choice, they chose to believe Satan and follow him.

Read Genesis 3:16–24 and Romans 5:12–13. What did the choices of Adam and Eve do to their lives? What did it do for our lives today?

If Satan is the father of lies, what is the way to defeat him?

Read John 8:32 and 14:6.

Jesus Christ is our answer to Satan's schemes. Satan is a liar, but Jesus is the truth. If we choose to follow Christ and believe in him, we can defeat Satan. We can block out his lies.

Who is Jesus?

> "He is the image of the invisible God, the firstborn over all creation. For by him all things were created: things in heaven and on earth, visible and invisible, whether thrones or powers or rulers or authorities; all things were created by him and for him. He is before all things, and in him all things hold together. And he is the head of the body, the church; he is the beginning and the firstborn from among the dead, so that in everything he might have the supremacy. For God was pleased to have all his fullness dwell in him, and through him to reconcile to himself all things, whether things on earth or things in heaven, by making peace through his blood, shed on the cross." Colossians 1:15–20.

How can you have the power of Jesus on your side? Read John 8:24. Believe in Jesus and accept him. He is the only way to be free of the sin and death that result from Satan's deception.

Now that you have worked through this assignment, what do you want to see as the next step?

John F. Gillette, Ph.D.

Our Spiritual Battles

> Be self-controlled and alert. Your enemy the devil prowls around like a roaring lion looking for someone to devour.
>
> *1 Peter 5:8*

christian counseling teaching tools

Who brings spiritual battles into our lives?

Christians face many spiritual battles. Satan desires that that we pursue our fleshly desires, and it is he who sits as the god of this world (Ephesians 2:1–13). Satan's prime objective is the defeat of God. For those of us who are Christians, that means Satan aims to defeat us as well. Satan's goal of defeating God is played out in the destruction of the lives of Christians. If you are a Christian, you are a target of Satan.

Jesus told his disciples, "I have given you authority to trample on snakes and scorpions and to overcome all the power of the enemy; nothing will harm you" (Luke 10:19). The word *power* can also be translated *authority*. Christ was telling his disciples that they had authority over the power of Satan, but not necessarily power over Satan himself.

As Christians, where does our power come from?

Read and meditate on Ephesians 1:18–23.

According to this passage, where does our power come from?

What is that power like?

How are where does Christ have power?

Where does Christ receive his power?

If you had that kind of power, how would your life be different?

When Christ was raised from the dead, the world witnessed the act of resurrection and the surrounding events as one of the greatest workings of God manifested in the Scriptures. Satan was defeated. All of this unleashing of God's might was for you and me, so that we could have victory over sin. What an exciting thought! The source of our authority over Satan is rooted in God and his power.

Pray a prayer like this for the next few mornings and see if you feel more of God's power in your life:

Lord, I accept my position. I acknowledge it to be at the right hand of the Father, and today, through the Holy Spirit, cause it to be a reality to me so that I might experience victory. My position has come through knowledge of Jesus Christ, a belief and acceptance of him, and an awareness of the conflict that we have with the enemy. Thank you, God, for the authority that I have in Christ Jesus!
Amen.

Now that you have worked through this assignment, what do you want to see as the next step?

John F. Gillette, Ph.D.

Our Spiritual Warfare

Submit yourselves, then, to God. Resist the devil, and he will flee from you.

James 4:7

christian counseling teaching tools

Christian living involves six areas that, when things are going well, are areas of strength.

Sufficiency (2 Corinthians 12:9)
But he said to me, "My grace is sufficient for you, for my power is made perfect in weakness." Therefore I will boast all the more gladly about my weaknesses, so that Christ's power may rest on me.

A Full Life (John 10:10)
The thief comes only to steal and kill and destroy; I have come that they may have life, and have it to the full.

The Life of a Conqueror (Romans 8:37)
No, in all these things we are more than conquerors through him who loved us.

Victory (1 Corinthians 15:57)
But thanks be to God! He gives us the victory through our Lord Jesus Christ.

Triumph (2 Corinthians 2:14)
But thanks be to God, who always leads us in triumphal procession in Christ and through us spreads everywhere the fragrance of the knowledge of him.

Holiness (Ephesians 1:3–5)
Praise be to the God and Father of our Lord Jesus Christ, who has blessed us in the heavenly realms with every spiritual blessing in Christ. For he chose us in him before the creation of the world to be holy and blameless in his sight. In love he predestined us to be adopted as his sons through Jesus Christ, in accordance with his pleasure and will—to the praise of his glorious grace, which he has freely given us in the One he loves.

Christian living also involves struggles. Sometimes struggles come into our lives (Romans 7:14–20). Sin brings about struggles, and we continually sin. Struggles come from within (flesh problems) and from without (world problems). And struggles come from the supernatural (evil spirit problems).

- You are still a Christian even if you are struggling with a serious sin problem (1 Corinthians 11:30–32; 1 John 2:1–2).
- You are still a Christian even if you are struggling a serious world problem (2 Timothy 4:10).
- You are still a Christian even if you are struggling with a serious demonic problem (1 Timothy 3:6–7).

Commands for Christian Living

Read James 4:7–8. What should a Christian do to resist problems?

Read 1 John 1:6–10. Confession is an important part of the solution to our problems. How does confession relate to submission?

Read Psalm 139:23–24. Confession is both personal and corporate. What do you need to confess personally?

Read Nehemiah 1:4–9. What confession needs to be made on a family level or church family level?

Read 2 Corinthians 7:9–11. How does repentance relate to submission?

Read Romans 12:1–2. How does commitment relate to submission?

RESIST THE DEVIL.

Resisting evil involves verbal confrontation based upon the truth of God's Word. It involves: faith, salvation, the Bible, and prayer.

Meditate on the following verses:

- Matthew 4:1–11
- Luke 4:1–13
- Ephesians 3:10–11
- Ephesians 6:16–18
- Revelation 12:11

Draw near to God. Sense his presence. Worship, praise, love, glorify. We have a defeated enemy (Acts 16:18; Hebrews 2:14).

Now that you have worked through this assignment, what do you want to see as the next step?

John F. Gillette, Ph.D.

OUR SUFFERING

I know whom I have believed, and am convinced that he is able to guard what I have entrusted to him for that day

2 Timothy 1:12

---

christian counseling teaching tools

Why must I suffer?

I have been told that God is absolutely good and infinitely loving. He is all-powerful. So why do I suffer if I am a product of his creative power and the focus of his infinite love? I don't understand!

Many people suffer.

What we often wish for when we are suffering is a "quick-fix," an instant cure. But God has permitted suffering. He knew that the plan he chose, even though it allows for sin and suffering, ultimately would bring about the greatest good and glory. Our suffering is directly related to the curse that came upon the earth as the result of sin. With sin came corruption, suffering, and death. This is not to say that every occurrence of suffering in our lives is direct punishment for our personal sins. The sooner we accept the reality that we are living in a fallen world with its suffering, the sooner we will be able to get on with living effectively.

In sickness and in health, let us remember that God is an all-knowing God. He is all-loving. Therefore, he will never do anything that is not for our good. We do not have to question God. Instead, we should ask him to search our hearts. If we are being stretched too far, he knows our limits. God will never test us beyond what we are able to bear. The Christian life is not easy, but God is faithful—nothing is too hard for him.

How can we cope with suffering?

It has helped me to study God's attributes. It is not possible to fully define or understand God, but we can gain confidence in our limited understanding. Look up the following verses related to the attributes of God.

Genesis 21:33   eternal
Isaiah 40:13–14   self-sufficient
Ephesians 1:3–14 supreme ruler
Revelation 19:6   controller of all things

Think Right!

Read Psalm 27:1. What does the fear of God do for you?

Read Hebrews 8:10. How can God's Word be a part of your life?

"What is impossible with men is possible with God."

I know where suffering comes from.
I know that God is in control.
I know that we are responsible for our actions.
I know that this life is nothing when compared with eternity.
I know God allows suffering to prepare us to:
> Comfort others
> Teach us to trust in him
> Turn our hearts toward heaven
> Bring about his glory
> Develop maturity
> Discipline us for sinful behavior
> Judge wickedness

Be intimate with God. A conscious, continuing fellowship will daily give you strength. A daily breathing out of sin through confession and breathing in of his presence is necessary. This involves self-examination with honesty. It involves confession and sensitivity to the truth. It involves submission and identification with the Lord. It involves asking and believing with thanksgiving.

Intimacy with God through Christ in the Holy Spirit is accomplished through constant trust. This trust provides that inner assurance that is needed to keep going.

It has helped me to know that the Holy Spirit makes intercession for me, along with Christ. When I am in turmoil, I am assured that I am not left to my own resources. The Holy Spirit keeps on helping me. He knows my needs, my very mind and heart. He intercedes to enable me to meet each crisis. He prays according to God's plans for my life.

John F. Gillette, Ph.D.

OUR SUFFICIENCY

That is why, for Christ's sake, I delight in weaknesses, in insults, in hardships, in persecutions, in difficulties. For when I am weak, then I am strong.

2 Corinthians 12:10

christian counseling teaching tools

Paul in 2 Corinthians 12 tells his readers that although difficult situations occurred in his life, he was strong in Christ. In fact, Paul says he "delights" in difficult situations. What could he possibly mean?

Previously in 2 Corinthians, Paul lists some of the difficult situations that had been part of his life. He mentions a list of horrible situations:

Imprisonment
Beatings
Stonings
Shipwrecks
Dangerous rivers
Bandits
Persecutions
Sleepless nights
Inclement weather
Lack of food and water

Not only was Paul in physical danger, he also was tormented by emotional pain.

Concern for the church
Rejection
Hated
Unloved
Betrayed
Unappreciated
Criticized
Falsely accused
Distrusted

What are some areas in your life that you consider "difficult" situations?

You can learn to handle your difficult situations by seeing where Paul's sufficiency lay. Paul's sufficiency was in Christ. No matter what happened, he was able to bear it with Christ on his side. Read 2 Corinthians 12:7–10. How did Paul come to know his sufficiency?

Starting point: Humility and inadequacy.

Paul knew that he was unable to do anything without Christ. Read John 15:5. What can you do without Christ? How does that affect your attitude toward difficult situations?

Second point: Dependence and initiative.

Paul asked God to take away his "thorn in the flesh" (see 2 Corinthians 12:8). When we ask for help from God, he will provide us with strength. What do you need strength to face?

Third point: Power indwelling

"My power is made perfect in weakness." God's power is most evident in our weaknesses. So we as rest and rely on God, his power is apparent in our lives.

Fourth point: Contentment

Paul is content with his troubles. Read James 1:2–4. How can you view situations that you face? How will you react to difficulties? Where will your power come from?

There is no promise of trouble-free living, only power to endure the trouble that is inevitable. God's grace is provided as we exercise humility, dependence, sufficiency, power, and contentment.

Write a prayer to God below. Thank him for your eternal inheritance, not the temporal things of this world. Trust him. Thank him for the difficult situations you face. Thank him that he is sufficient.

Now that you have worked through this assignment, what do you want to see as the next step?

John F. Gillette, Ph.D.

OVERCOMING ADDICTIONS

> The one who is in you is greater than the one who is in the world.
>
> *1 John 4:4*

christian counseling teaching tools

WHAT IS ADDICTION?

The dictionary defines addiction as "the compulsive need for and use of a habit-forming substance."

Our mind can trick us into becoming addicted to many different things. Whenever we think we can't live without something, we are victims of addiction. Can you know you are addicted?

Where are you in your mind-tricks? Check what applies to you.

Self-deception

Denial _____
Depression _____
Rationalization _____
Hiding _____

Delaying Tactics

Giving up _____
Handling it _____
Breaking down _____

Collision

Facing the issue _____
Retreating from the issue _____

What do you feel is an addiction for you?

Assume responsibility for yourself and daily put into practice these steps.

1. Limit your thoughts on the situation.

2. Share your thoughts with supporters.

3. Refocus your thoughts—get into the Bible-reading habit.

4. Know yourself

5. Motivate yourself.

6. Teach yourself.

Read the following texts and write down the key thoughts to overcoming Satan's temptations and schemes.

Matthew 4:1–11

Mark 1:12–13

Luke 4:1–13

Stand firm.
Don't rationalize. Meet the challenge.

Decide to win.
Don't retreat. Use your will.

Respond with Scripture.
Don't rely on self. Be in harmony with God's will.

DAILY AFFIRMATION RESPONSE

Jesus responded to Satan's attacks with confidence and strength. You can learn from Jesus' example.

1. Accept the Word of God as your final authority. Believe God, not your feelings, not your circumstances. If you have repented and believed in Jesus as your Savior and Lord, you are complete in him.

2. Daily choose by faith to live in the enabling power of the Holy Spirit. Through the crucifixion and resurrection of Jesus Christ, you can do it.

3. Cooperate actively with the ministry of the indwelling Holy Spirit by being obedient to God.

4. Deliberately choose to respond to God. Honestly surrender to God and his Word. Sincerely face your need and make the correct decision of obedience and complete trust.

Now that you have worked through this assignment, what do you want to see as the next step?

John F. Gillette, Ph.D.

THE SURE CURE

If you hold to my teaching, you are really my disciples. Then you will know the truth, and the truth will set you free.

John 8:31–32

christian counseling teaching tools

Have you become a slave to your compulsions?

Have you become addicted to life-destroying patterns?

Have you become brainwashed that there is a quick-fix for your problems?

Real hope for human freedom and growth is found in God's grace. It's not a mystery. The possibility is full of free-flowing power from God through Jesus Christ and guidance from the Holy Spirit. It begins with the Scripture from John: "If you."
    We must respond with our heads and hearts to the gospel. If you are seeking peace and hope, you can find that through making a **confession** of faith. A confession means an agreement or belief that Jesus Christ died on the cross for you. By his death our sins are taken away and because of his resurrection, we are able to live in victory. By relinquishing all for God, we dedicate our lives to the victory that comes from our belief. True liberation comes when the heart says "Yes" to God's call of "Follow me."
    Once you confess Christ is God, true freedom will follow.

Let's examine John 8:31–32.

"If you hold to my teaching"
What is God's teaching? See Psalm 119:1–2; 2 Timothy 3:16–17.

What does it mean to hold to God's teaching?

What does the word *commitment* mean to you?

After you confess your belief in Christ, your **commitment** to him must deepen. Confession is followed by a deep craving for God's Word. How do you build a relationship with Christ? You absorb the Bible into every activity of life. As you depend on God to guide your actions through his Word, you will find your destructive actions turn into constructive actions. Become addicted to God's Word. Your life will transform as you obey it and live it.

"You will know the truth"
What is the truth? See John 14:6.

After confession and commitment comes change. When you believe in Christ and commit to follow him, a changed life will result. You stop focusing on the temporary obsessions and focus of your former life and begin to ask yourself: "What will last for eternity? What is really important in life? What are real values in life?"

Your old behavior will begin to change as you begin to make right decisions. When failures and struggles come, you learn that as you focus on the words of God, you can overcome any trial or temptation. As you recognize God's intervention, you will begin the last step toward true freedom.

WHAT DOES FREEDOM MEAN TO YOU?

"The truth will set you free"

Everything we do involves some kind of dedication. When we try to reform a troublesome addiction, our struggle is dedicated to minimizing the pain that addiction causes others and us. When the truth of Jesus becomes our reality, our struggle becomes consecrated. **Consecration** means "dedicated" or "set apart to God." God is intimately involved in our struggles. His grace sets us free. God powers our energy and effort!

In the spiritual process called discipleship, we become leaders on our road to recovery by exercising responsibility through the help of the Holy Spirit.

How do you want to respond to God's call to be involved in your life?

How are you moving through the stages mentioned in this handout (commitment, change, and consecration)?

What will you need to do to move to the next stage?

Now that you have worked through this assignment, what do you want to see as the next step?

John F. Gillette, Ph.D.

OUR TESTIMONY

I have set the LORD always before me.
Because he is at my right hand,
I will not be shaken.

Psalm 16:8

christian counseling teaching tools

After we become Christians, we often discover that some Bible verses become our favorites. When we talk with others about our Christian experience, we share those verses. When we share our "testimony" with others, we tell them about our beliefs. We share some of our favorite verses.

Read 1 Corinthians 15:1–4. These verses declare a decision. With careful study of the evidence, we can have confidence that the Bible is God's Word. There is no doubt in my mind that it is. Let it speak for itself. Find a quite place and begin to read it. You will be surprised—it will touch your heart.

How will you respond to 1 Corinthians 15:1–4? Are these verses representative of your testimony?

Here is what I believe. This is my testimony:

God, the supernatural being who created the heavens and the earth, loved us and gave his Son to die for us. Jesus Christ, the Son of God, became our substitute for the penalty of sin. We all have sinned. We have inherited sinful nature because of the disobedience of Adam and Eve back in the garden of Eden. As a result, we do not measure up to God's standards. The only way to be accepted is through believing that the punishment that Christ took upon himself is what we deserved. He took upon himself the judgement which had been meant for humanity. We have been forgiven and set free by God when we believe that he died for us. In Christ's resurrection, the believer has power to do what God wants.

Let's look at Psalm 16:8. Think about your own testimony in light of these verses.

"I have set the Lord always before me."
What is God in relation to your life? Is he front and center? Or is he back in a closet somewhere? Your relationship with God is an important part of your testimony.

"Because he is at my right hand"
After receiving Christ as our Savior, he became our Lord. We are to obey his commands. The Bible says to walk in Christ, to put on mercy, kindness, humbleness of mind, meekness, and long-suffering. Read Colossians 3:12–14. What are our lives supposed to look like in light of our relationship with Christ?

"I will not be shaken"
God's power and presence ultimately climax with his peace in our lives. Psalm 128:1 says, "Blessed are all who fear the LORD, who walk in his ways." Fear is two-fold and represents awe and reverence. The result is trust and confidence. When we fear God, we do not cringe before him. Instead, a satisfying peace comes over us.

Faith is primarily a decision to entrust ourselves to something or someone. We have learned the facts concerning our sin, and it demands a personal response. We have to make a decision to believe what God has to say and to trust Jesus Christ.

Where are you in your faith journey? Do you have a testimony to share with others? Answer the following questions, and from your answers, develop your own testimony.

- Who is God?
- Who is Jesus Christ?
- What did God do for all people through Christ?
- What practical affect does this knowledge have on your life?
- What do you want others to know about your relationship with God?

John F. Gillette, Ph.D.

OUR TRIALS

No temptation has seized you except what is common to man. And God is faithful; he will not let you be tempted beyond what you can bear. But when you are tempted, he will also provide a way out so that you can stand up under it.

1 Corinthians 10:13

christian counseling teaching tools

The Exposition

"No temptation"
The words here can mean a trial. Trials take many forms: hatred, hunger, sleeplessness, pain, misunderstanding, discouragement.
Or it can mean testing. This testing can help you grow in grace.
Or it can mean a temptation, which is what Satan uses to weaken us.

How we handle temptation is dependant on what we think, and how we act and react.

What is a temptation in your life?

"Common to man"
Your situation is not unique. God's promise is to help you in any situation.

"God is faithful"
We will not be tested beyond our capacity to endure. If we keep this truth in our minds, our attitudes will become right, and our behavior will change. Our minds can be renewed by focusing on the truth.

"Beyond what you can bear"
Others have endured and come through. Read Romans 7:15–25. We can overcome our struggles by having our minds focused on the truth.

The Enablement
- Put limits on your thoughts. Do not feed your old, destructive habits.
- Avoid the triggers that lead to you to temptations.
- Identify the root problems.
- Reestablish values. Renew your mind daily.
- Share your thoughts. Talk to your church family; join a group.
- Disassociate from your temper. Flee from it!
- Gain an accountability source. Find some dedicated spiritual friends.
- Refocus your thoughts, feelings, desires, hunger, behaviors. Get into the Bible-reading habit and pray every day.
- Follow a solid nutritional program to rebuild your body.
- Change regular patterns. Identify dangerous behaviors.
- Get motivated. Reward yourself for doing well.

The Escape
- Know yourself. What is holding on to your life? Admit your weaknesses.
- Seek renewal. Start with repentance and continue in obedience.
- Build a strong life-context. Are you devoted to doctrine, fellowship, service, prayer, worship?
- Know your enemy. He creates doubt. He manipulates and seduces.
- Motivate yourself for right living. This world is not your home. God can use you in many ways here if you ask for his guidance.
- Beware of your strengths. Concentrate on your gifts.
- Shift your energy away from temptation. Redeem the time.
- Don't' feed your cravings. Regularly eat less and reject any obsessions.
- Develop good habits. Learn to say NO.
- Teach yourself by letting God get your attention. Try to internalize his thoughts.
- Run from temptation. Don't compromise your integrity.
- Be courageous.

The Endurance

- Admit when you need help.
- Establish a life in God.
- Have accountable relationships.
- List things that are struggles for you. Then admit them, repent of failures and forgive yourself.
- Enter into prayer.
- Dare to share with others.

Read Proverbs 24:16 for encouragement.

You can do it! Victory involves a daily relationship with Jesus Christ.

Read Galatians 5:22. Self-control is possible.

Rev. John F. Gillette, Ph.D.

WARFARE

"the day of evil"

Ephesians 6:13

---

christian counseling teaching tools

Demonic assault is nothing to be taken lightly. Spiritual warfare is real. When you are faced with an attack from Satan, look at the messy situation and picture God the salvager right in the middle of it.

Read Ephesians 6:10–18.

Meditate on these suggestions.

Be gripped by God's truths.

Know who you are.

Believe that you are ready for anything.

Stay cool!

Exercise hope.

Let God have his say.

Rest in the warfare.

As you look back at the previous 7 thoughts, ask yourself how each section applies to you. Then write an affirmation from each section.

Other responses to consider:

Memorize Scripture and recite what you are memorizing each day:

Proverbs 24:16
Romans 8:32
1 Thessalonians 5:8

Every week write a letter of victory, where you record the positive steps you have seen in your life.

Notes taken from Ken Koeman, "Standing Your Ground Under Satan's Attack." The Banner, October 15, 1990, p. 6.

Now that you have some knowledge about warfare, be proactive. How will you respond to the next attack? Write a possible scenario.

What will the attack be like?

What part of Ephesians 6:10–18 will apply to this situation?

How will you put the word of God into action in this situation?

Now that you have worked through this assignment, what do you want to see as the next step?

John F. Gillette, Ph.D.

OUR WORSHIP

Let us hold unswervingly to the hope we profess, for he who promised is faithful. And let us consider how we may spur one another on toward love and good deeds. Let us not give up meeting together, as some are in the habit of doing, but let us encourage one another—and all the more as you see the Day approaching.

Hebrews 10:23–25

christian counseling teaching tools

Why go to church?

Here are some thoughts:
- Because we are in a organic union with its head.
- Because we are related to its members.
- Because the organized church is recognized in the New Testament.
- Because the church is a self-developing body.
- Because of the new resurrection fellowship day.
- Because we are one in accord in witnessing.
- Because we are to give our tithes and gifts in obedience.
- Because it is our duty.

Reread Hebrews 10:23–25. Then read 2 Thessalonians 2:1. There is no place for isolation regarding the believer. We are called to gather with others. Some reasons we are to gather is to exhort, encourage, and admonish each other. The day when Christ will return is approaching. Shouldn't we find ourselves together in obedience to his will?

"There are two ways of stopping a wind-up clock. You can smash it, or you can let it run down. There are two ways of doing away with churches. You can destroy them, or you can ignore them. If we are going to fight for the liberty of worship, we ought to make some use of that liberty."

LET'S SEE WHAT THE BIBLE SAYS ABOUT WORSHIP.

Read John 4:23. What has happened to true worshipers today?

Read Isaiah 55:9. Have we shaped our concept of God to fit our own understanding of him? How have you seen evidence of this in the church?

Read Psalm 95:6. What will it take for you to worship God? What will you have to do?

Read Revelation 4:10. What is a "crown"? What will you throw before God?

Read Revelation 4:11. How can you tell God about what you feel for him?

Our response to worship is a part of our relationship with Christ. Now that you understand what worship is, how can you worship God? What is in your life that is keeping you from worshiping God?

Below write out your response to what you have learned about God and worship.

Choose a Psalm that seems worshipful and meditate upon it. Then respond with a psalm of your own, written to God.

John F. Gillette, Ph.D.

About the Author

John F. Gillette's story begins and ends with a song he sang in his childhood, "His Very Own, Wonderful Grace in His Word is made known, chosen by the Father, purchased by the Son, sealed by the Spirit, I am his very own." His desire every day is to glorify the Lord Jesus Christ in health and in sickness. He has learned every moment needs to be in God's presence.

Divine dialogue is a developmental process. He has been a lifelong student of the Scriptures. It is easy to fail the standards of God but he has an inner passion that he calls "the holy urge" to encourage him to go forward. His studies have been in the liberal arts but always guided through his biblical deep rooted foundation. His graduate research has been in religion and leadership.

He has served Jesus Christ since his childhood with diversity, independence and confidence in education, pastorate and leadership. His pastoral health care discovery series was published to help himself and minister to others that are having struggles in making spiritual, psychological and physiological adjustments.

More Books in the Series:

Discovering God's Sufficiency
Going Beyond Ourselves and Experiencing the Supernatural
Pastoral Health Care—Part One

Can anyone fix our troubles? The answer is 'yes.' How do we conquer our trials? We have to affirm God's intervention. We have to accept God's indwelling. We have to make some adjustments through God's illumination. We can experience God's power, presence and peace.

Discovering God's Love
Confirming God's love through the evidence of historical facts
Pastoral Health Care—Part Two

We can obtain strength to conquer through a knowledge of the 'Gospels' and receiving Jesus Christ into our hearts. The New Testament books of history give evidence of God's love. Through his love and faith, we are able to be strengthened, experience his support and become steadfast.

Available at www.schulerbooks.com/chapbook-press

Discovering God's Heart
Feeling God's heart pulse is our daily challenge
Pastoral Health Care—Part Five

We have to practice the principles in the pastoral health care meditation method. We can handle any situation through thinking biblically. The spirit, soul and body are involved. Therefore, a holistic approach has to take place.

Available at www.schulerbooks.com/chapbook-press

Discovering God's Counsel
Applying his spiritual solution to meet difficult trials
Pastoral Health Care—Part Three

Dark days can be life threatening. We have to develop an adequate level of spiritual, psychological and physiological adjustments. We can live with confidence in God's sufficiency.

Discovering God's Kingdom
Finding a way to understand ourselves in a complex world
Pastoral Health Care—Part Four

Dealing with life, death, heaven and eternity with God's perspective is necessary. It involves a personal decision of belief, trust and faith. Knowledge and commitment will bring comfort and security. The eternal destiny directive will provide the way.

www.ingramcontent.com/pod-product-compliance
Lightning Source LLC
Chambersburg PA
CBHW070101080526
44586CB00013B/1145